THE KIOSK ON THE BRINK

By the same author:

The Sirocco Room (1991)

THE KIOSK
ON THE BRINK

Jamie McKendrick

Oxford   New York
OXFORD UNIVERSITY PRESS

Oxford University Press, Walton Street, Oxford OX2 6DP
Oxford New York Toronto
Delhi Bombay Calcutta Madras Karachi
Kuala Lumpur Singapore Hong Kong Tokyo
Nairobi Dar es Salaam Cape Town
Melbourne Auckland Madrid
and associated companies in
Berlin Ibadan

Oxford is a trade mark of Oxford University Press

© Jamie McKendrick 1993

First published in Oxford Poets
as an Oxford University Press paperback 1993

British Library Cataloguing in Publication Data
Data available

Library of Congress Cataloging in Publication Data
McKendrick, Jamie, 1955–
The kiosk on the brink / Jamie McKendrick.
p. cm.
I. Title.
PS6063.C544K56 1993 821'.914—dc20 92-34890
ISBN 0-19-283118-6 (pbk.)

3 5 7 9 10 8 6 4

Printed in Hong Kong

For Jenny and Lee Holland

ACKNOWLEDGEMENTS

Acknowledgements are due to the editors of the following: *Gairfish*; *New Internationalist*; *Oxford Poetry*; *Poetry Book Society Anthology (1991–92)*; *Times Literary Supplement*; and to the Pitt-Rivers Museum, Oxford where several of these poems were exhibited.

The author gratefully acknowledges the assistance of the Arts Council for a Bursary in 1991.

I am indebted to Xon de Ros for help with the Quevedo and Machado versions.

salendo e rigirando la montagna
che drizza voi che 'l mondo fece torti.

Purgatorio, XXIII

CONTENTS

I

Under the Volcano 13
User 14
The Vulcanologist 15
The Earth's Rind 16
Ye Who Enter In 17
Back from the Brink 18
Bradyseism 19
Sky Nails 20
The Seismographical Survey 21
Et in Orcadia Ego 22
The Wrong Side 23
The Agave 25
Loss 26
Tinnitus 27
Terminus 28
The Crystal Sky 29
Windrose 30

II

ledge 33
on the volcano 34
flood 35
il tremoto 36
lengths of air 37
hortus conclusus 38

III

The Return 41
Black Sounds 42
Source 43
Sirensong 44
Skin Deep 45
Uroboros 46
Frankenstein's Pre-Natal Recollections 47
Stood Up 48
He drinks precious wine with flies in 49
Home Thoughts 50

The Master Stroke   51
suspicion   52
sleight of hand   53
mortal remains   54
Inheritance   55
A Small Flag   57

I

UNDER THE VOLCANO

Between the Devil's Viaduct and the deep blue sea,
any darkened patch or nook will do,
they gather for the rites of youth
—a soluble nectar that arrives
from nowhere, like a boat in the port.

Incendi dolosi. A bronze light worries
the night sky where the hillside
consumes itself. Those
wanting compensation tie
a burning brand to a trapped bird's foot

so where the bird alights in terror
flames spread. No one's
the wiser as when the camorra
firebomb a discotheque or bar.
You sense the sulphur under the earth's crust.

The cortège follows the boy
they found in the Park of Springtime,
his forearm dandling a syringe.
Between the viaduct and the seafront
you crush the brittle flowers underfoot.

Incendi dolosi: arson

USER

Your presence is hungry and highpitched,
the note of nails screed down a blackboard
snatching the backbone in a fist of quills.
You hear it yourself and want to escape
frantic and headlong, a wasp in a jamjar.

Under the nightshade of a parasol,
light lacquered mauve and gold, you summon
friends in prison or overdosed and dead
without their lady of the lamp. You've lost
count of the times you've given the kiss of life;

still working as a local pool attendant,
weren't you once a lifeguard by the ocean?
Airmails come from the home you left behind you
but the past you can't put there—it plagues you
like a swarm of a hornets, a coiffure of fire.

Your dealers use the tradesman's entrance.
Then you wear a halo of candyfloss,
a glutinous helmet, lighter than air.
Coming down, you long to be forgiven and forget.
And the next morning crashes into you.

THE VULCANOLOGIST

Athanasius   Kircher
having   completed   his
key work on Coptic grammar
(and rightly linked it to the
hieroglyphs)   left   the   cardinals
in Rome and set about his Latin tract
on volcanoes. He visited Etna and Vesuvius,
and Vesuvius he entered, let down the inner
walls by lengths of rope, growing smaller and
smaller like a bug on a thread tacked to the sky's
vault with tiny pins of adamant. There he swung past
fumaroles with poison yellow plumes, abseiling through
gardens of brimstone and red cinders. He saw the vestibule
he knew would lead to a vast network of subterranean flames,
lakes of bitumen and burning conduits threading land and ocean
from Iceland to Patagonia. In his book he mapped fire's empire and
its outposts, the whole racked body of Hephaestos, whose molten heart
we build our spindly cities on, and plant and tend our perishable groves

THE EARTH'S RIND

The Earth's rind is finer, more close-grained
than an apple's skin—if we assume
the material world is not
just an illusion. Nonetheless
we're stuck in this nothing, if such
we admit it is, up to our necks.
The pessimists say that what sticks
us here is everything we've made
to replace the gods. But the old God's
still faithful followers assert
this substitution didn't take.
Perhaps He'll come, they say, in person
to prize us from the magma limb
by limb. So we live and are
a double life, even if the self-
adoring would choose only one.
O mother Earth, O Heaven
of celestial beings—it's this
that's the problem,
that makes us mad and shriller than
a bird in lime.

(after E. Montale)

YE WHO ENTER IN

To plumb the depths of hell and meet
ministers, saladins and scholars,
Marilyn Monroe and Cleopatra,
the latter naked as the day they died;
to give audience where you please
and where you don't to curl your lip
or deftly rabbit-punch a kidney
sure that your arm is power-assisted.
To be steered about by someone who just
happens to be Virgil, and you like his poems.
To write as a chisel writes on rock
so every phrase you write resounds forever:
ABANDON ALL HOPE. . . . You first.
No really I insist please after you.

(after Antonio Machado)

BACK FROM THE BRINK

like the time I went to sleep while driving
and began to dream that there was something
wrong with the car—the noise it made
was ominous like liquid looking

for a hairline crack, some brittle chink
it meant to rip wide open or explode
so I drove it in my dream to the mechanic's
—a shoggly booth he'd roofed with zinc—

where he looked it over, shook his head
and told me that the problem was electric
though luckily his friend across the road
(and here I must have steered across the road)

would fix it. But his friend said what I'd need
was a real maestro in hydraulics
—and one with wings at least if, hearing Greek,
I hadn't slammed my foot down on the brake.

BRADYSEISM

for Michael and Posy O'Neill

All I had was in that crate, its death
creak the tremor of a fallen sparrow,
its nose in a ditch by a sliproad between
X and Y—an X I couldn't return to
and a Y I'd no mind and still less means
to arrive at. But the lamp-post was only
a few degrees off vertical so things
were looking up—if the earth might please
stop shaking up and down, the fields
kinking in small ashen troughs and crests
on their way to where the sky rightly
would have no more of them. Pozzuoli
of the heart!—those listing columns sunk
like toadstools in a grey mephitic lake . . .

I took a train which stitched its head
through the stone heart of Europe
—the wrong train. Snow everywhere
as though God had got tired of His landscapes.
A Frenchwoman with a silver cloud of hair
helped me see how all was for the best
now I had met her and could hear of Him:
'What shall it profit a man to win
the whole world, and lose . . . ?' Life, for her,
was full of these fruitful coincidences
hanging on bare branches. I spent the night
at Metz in the station waiting-room beside
a tramp who snored like a man of property
—gently distending and subsiding—
and just had time to visit the cathedral
humping my riches in a rucksack.
In my breast pocket, quakily-written, an address
of the Bible Mission—somewhere to head for.

SKY NAILS

That first day, to break me in,
my hardened comrades
sent me scampering like a marmoset
from the topmost parapet

to the foreman's hut
for a bag of sky nails.
The foreman wondered which precise
shade of blue I had in mind.

It's still sky nails I need today
with their faint threads
and unbreakable heads

that will nail anything
to nothing
and make it stay.

THE SEISMOGRAPHICAL SURVEY

Crumbling the tarmac into treacly clods
tufts of weed were using their green levers
on the disused airfield we drove across
to load our jeep up from the magazine
—that padlocked booth among the bullrushes
stacked with boxes of waxed cardboard sticks
and fuses trailing nervous wires . . .
We'd start where yesterday's fresh boreholes
lipped with screws of clay
made ten yard strides across Derbyshire
then stop beside each hole and blow it up.
I tamped the 1 lb. stick of dynamite
with a nine foot copper-ended pole
and fixed the fusewires to the detonator
which Arthur plunged so that the thump and spray
would surface as a heartbeat on the graph
in the technician's van which followed us
dark-windowed, white, a kind of ambulance.
And casualties occurred
though they were after something under us;
I never found out whether coal or oil
but Arthur's guess was that they found fuck all.
Day after day we'd trample through and cancel
field after field of corn rape barley pasture
and the odd headhigh field of sunflowers
and in our wake we sowed a line of craters
and echoes beaking down through soil and bedrock
and sods and divots falling in slow-motion.

The last day we bumped into this farmer
sleepily trudging through a field of his
balancing two offcuts of one coathanger
bent into right-angles.
After we'd shed our loaded shoulderbags
he showed us how to hold those L-shaped wires
lightly, how they made an X
above the water-channels we took on trust
then gradually uncrossed as we walked on
and how this other way with our own hands
we answered to those echoes underground.

ET IN ORCADIA EGO

Having heard the Orkneys were like Eden
we sold up everything and bought a farm.
A subsistence farm, I called it. There wasn't sun
enough for solar panels—the rays fell
at such an oblique angle, it was clear
they were heading for somewhere else,
some kinder place with trees. All round the year
the big winds tore about with wasteful power.
I felt that just by being there
I was tilting at windmills. Did I have to
build them as well? Since then I've often thought
if we'd run the waterpipes beneath the henshit
like smoky lava on the floor of the coop
we could have had hot water winterlong.

The last straw was a goat-breeding project.
Hoping the meat might sell, I'd bought
this Anglo-Nubian billy to beget
a nation and populate our land. I left him
tethered to a mulberry shrub . . . when God
stumbled upon the body of Abel
in the murderous quiet of the day
and sent Cain off to chew the bitter cud
he must have felt as I felt in that empty place.
The farm pony was looking darkly innocent
and the kid had withdrawn into his yellow gaze
—the colour made me think of Nile mud—
his jaw stove in by the pony's hoof.
All attempts to heal or tend him failed
and, though neither I nor Anne could keep it down,
we ended eating our last chance to stay.

THE WRONG SIDE

They fled the village when the mountainside
loosed a hail of boulders through their roofs. I stayed
in the one house left standing, a guest house
in a ghost town of cracked jambs and gaping doorways.
The man I shared with was unfortunately mad.
Rage and soft-spokenness, the poles he swung between,
were inseparable as the two chained sticks
he whirled about his head for martial exercise.
The generator at the back hummed like an iron locust
that would take off one day and turn the sky black.

Too good to be true (neither her strong point)
she arrived one morning but was followed.
Goats chewed the shadows of the rock and gazed
with proprietorial sarcasm
and planted themselves in my path to watch me
hesitate. On either side the vipers generated:
slack, small, untied like black boot laces,
their heads just big enough to hold one thought . . .

The kitchen had a noble view
of the circle of mountains that hemmed us in,
the air tasselled with heat and a viaduct
exerting itself above a riverbed
now dusty as a crater or a grate.
Straight down from that window was a sheer drop
into an elderberry wilderness—just one wrong foot,
a footfall, a rockfall, a word at the earth's core
would have had us head over heels in roots
and treetops, crashing through a valley of shadows.

The shadow of her breasts was nard and henna,
her lap a garden of elderberries
but my time was up and a car came for her.
Each day I walked to the new village where the old village
had regrouped, with its one-eyed bar and square
in the middle of which was a palm tree up to its chin
in white dust. I watched a chained goat on the slope
trying, without finesse, to befriend a hen
and coping with rejection time and again.
Then there was the station where some trains would stop

for practice I supposed. Or to catch their breath.
The lines led off to somewhere I'd begun
long before to lose faith in. By the blind ticket booth
a sign spoke four languages. The English read:
IT IS FORBIDDEN TO CROSS THE TOACKS.
That summer I came to know the Toacks
—with their roots hooked under the earth's crust.
On the right side of them you'd never guess
they even existed but from where I was
they were too deep to fathom and too tall to cross.

THE AGAVE

also called aloe, maguey, the century plant,
only seems to flourish where
an inch would launch it into space

on cliffs and ledges and descents
beside the prickly pears that crouch
in their hairsuits like luscious grudges.

Saw-toothed, sword-shaped, its fleshy leaves
are carved with hearts and hard-ons
by agile Orlandos.

After twenty, sometimes thirty years,
out of the powerhouse of its rootstock
from which the Aztecs brewed

their pulque and clear-eyed mescal,
it sprouts a lone stem limbed with bright
umbelliferous panicles

twenty, sometimes thirty foot tall
and at a rakish angle to the rock
then dies to leave the coastline

studded with the charred masts
and gutted decks of an armada.

LOSS

If what you hear is like a field
and the height of a lark above it
then the field has dwindled and the wind
bells on the razor wire around
the verge beyond which nothing
but the pointless din of outer space,
the addled Muzak of the spheres,
gets through to you. Acoustic junk.
The earth itself begins to hum
with the infinitesimal tunnelling
of umpteen holts and vaults and brood halls
and the sky each dawn is lower than
the day before as though wound down
like a press-head on a worm-screw
where once you woke and heard the threads
of birdsong trailed from hedge to hedge
as clear and intricately round
as a palm-bark epic in Telugu.

TINNITUS

The rustle of foil, a tide of pins, a wave
which never breaking
crinkles from the far side of the brink

and inches nearer with its crest
of decibels and wreckage under which
still you catch the cars diminishing, phrase

after phrase of the evening bird
fainter each time but holding out
from a twig upon a tree within a wood.

TERMINUS

Io ero tra color che son sospesi

Hanging on the hours like heliotropes
we have taken root where we set foot;
the sun favours our recreations
and salt in the seawind glazes us over
with a tan, a patina, taken for health.

We greet each other with averted eyes
and shipwrecked smiles. Otherwise
indulge in the stern vice of vivisection
and self-portraiture: exiles who left
for no reason with no reason to return.

THE CRYSTAL SKY

The city of glass was throwing stones
of glass at the neighbouring city of stone.
Then nothing happened worth reporting.

I lived in an outcrop cube of thinnest glass,
a little showcase of bad habits
—unspeakable things I did at night

waiting for the Reprisal, the moon aqueous
rose-coloured, almost within reach.
The person I like to think of as my friend

suffered my late calls detecting
an illness too limpid for the textbooks.
A glass tide tinkled on the hull

of the receiver, its echoing obsidian.
Our voices rocked on the pauses, becalmed.
That pipette of plantfood had made the agave

sprout two feet in one day—it was too much
the way it swigged litres of fresh water
as if survival was so important.

Between the moon and my see-through roof
a purple storm was blowing the dust
of some previous war into the waste spaces.

Then in the brittle hour before dawn
it occurred to me there might might there not
still be time to set my house in order.

WINDROSE

When we threw caution to the winds, the city
was the city of winds which blew from the four points, the eight quarters
of the windrose, a star which creaked and skittered on its hinge
and reared dustdevils—helices, rootless, footloose, almost human—

and a palm frond swept the public garden paths
like a bird feigning lameness—shuffle, hop, another shuffle—
while a plinth of sunlight turned the sea's roof turquoise
and tides lashed the concrete calthrops of the breakwater.

On a calm day once from Posillipo I saw
the sea, way out, extrude a pillar of salt, a corkscrew
that tapped the deep and lifted shoals to rain down on our roofs
like wingless birds who'd flown through sheer assumption.

II

ledge

The mountain would have crashed on top of us
but it needed to unlace its concrete stays
and the wire mesh that caged its overhang.

Lilies splashed with fire from the underworld
grew in a niche beneath the barn owl's nest
—all night we heard her catastrophic wheezing

and the even breathing of the tideless sea
down where the steps expired, tired of counting,
of footsoles, heels, of having to be steps

so far below while up above as far
the coast road curled and shed its cast-offs
for the morning on the balcony:

a ripe fig, a hairclip, a fag-end, a feather
and a faint premonitory sprinkling of stones.

on the volcano

For years in the shadow of the mountain
we'd never thought to cast our shadows on it,
to peep down into it from up above . . .

slag and clinkers; an afterthought that still
plagues the earth about her final form;
a verruca; a welt; a peak of hell

erected in the midst of paradise.
Fumes idled up the inner walls
as we stopped at the kiosk on the brink

vending cans of molten sugar, dreadful trade,
then wound back down by the parched red track
to the car park where the Gypsy woman sat

with those chunks of pyrite, fool's gold, fire
cooled, cast and cubed in the dire forge.

flood

The mountain dug its heels into the draff
that ran from its sides in ropes of gravel
as the black pearls of rain hit off the rock.

Then the sea moved in to meet the mountain's flow
and overstepped the concrete mole and wrecked
the beach huts, the football pitch, the sandwich stall

and scaled the doorsteps and the window sills
where it came to rest. Along that level
the bay and the square were a seamless cope

the tops of the tallest cars kept just above
while their owners circled them in rowboats
and, half its height, the square's one palm tree

rode the ripples through that inland sea
with the air of a battered periscope.

il tremoto

Inside the mountain earth begins to move
its joints and spring the links that pegged it down
—the fans of schist, the chocks and wedges of

feldspar and chert. A daylight owl screws back
from rock that spilling derelicts her nest
then quiet plugs the ear, a twist of wax.

Behind the quiet a core of silence hums
until earth moves again—this time in earnest:
dumb matter's rigid-tongued delirium

wrung at the verge of the crack that gapes at
the heart of things, that widens the Norman watchtower
from its sunken gateway to the parapet

as the tide uncoils. This means in Purgatory
a soul pinned to the rock has broken free

lengths of air

The mountain had its shoulders in the cloud
it kept its head above, rich folds of cloud
with tassels spilling round a clump of rock.

Above the cloud a village like a wasps' nest
in fractured soapy pinks and crusted honey
hung on to nothing by a thread

and from its topmost balcony a woman
let out the rope that let her basket down
past the cloud, the winding road, the lemon groves

in their black nets and down the mountainside
until it reached sea-level where I knelt
and found inside the photo and the note.

I trembled at that nakedness and read:
here I am on my bed inlaid with lapis

hortus conclusus

The Reptilarium has parked under the palm tree
like an Ark on wheels, a seething caravan
it costs no more than the news to enter.

Tomorrow we can read about the world
but today we'll wander back to origin
and see through glass what took Eve's breath away

and gave it back quickened. The sleepy snakes
lie wreathed around themselves or slither through
the hoops of their own skin, their hanks of hemp.

A tongue or a mouse's tail retracts within
the lipless smile of a green tree python.
Such heavy necklaces! So far from Eden!

The driver counts the coins into his tin.
The sun curls its last rays round the mountain.

III

THE RETURN

This is the indelible place you lived in.
There's no mistaking the scales of moonlight
on the stucco though the fertile gutters

are only shadows, some windows have been lost,
some scarred with fire and the kiosk selling
cut watermelons and contraband tobacco

has lapsed. You try to ignore the gaps around
your memory palace: the statue of Neptune
that served to hide a patch of turquoise sea;

the convent which in your time was a brothel.
A team of builders from the coast are still
plastering the vaults of the vestibule

which even with scaffolding are out of reach.
Now you take the street inside the palace
and turn left down some worn steps into night

where the walls jostle you and brush your arm
with whitewash. You stand at the iron door
to calm yourself then turn the iron key

and face the next door. You're sure that everything
will now be as it was and hardly look
till you reach the long room: pale green damask

is pouring off the bed in dark green folds.
The balcony is frail and higher than you thought
but looks down on the unchanged saffron flowers

of the pomegranate tree. Late summer comes.
The beige trunk, twisting, leans its topmost branch
onto the rail and offers you the last fruit,

its rind burst by the crush of cells,
and holding it out to light your way you leave
again determined to mislay the key.

BLACK SOUNDS

My guide was an urchin whom I chose
in preference to some scowling bandits
who tried to trip him as we passed—but how

had he learnt the dynasties and rituals
of the ancient and the recent troglodytes
who'd scored the bleached heights with a comb of cells?

With shards of pottery and pomegranate seeds
he explained how every year Persephone
has found her way down to the underworld

guided by the warbling of some nightbird
then retraced her steps by letting that coil unwind
which her descent had wound so tight inside her.

We entered dark interiors through white sockets
where the light would strain to turn a corner
but faint within a footstep of the doorstep.

At last we mounted the cablecar that fell
through the hanging gardens of the chasm:
bits of where we'd lived were scattered

on lovely terraces and families huddled
on creaking boughs under polythene.
Was that my cousin hanging by her heels?

The sky skipped like chips of phosphorus
in a bowl of water and oil seeped
through cracked earth to the watertable.

From where the monks had once drawn water
far down there on the valley's floor I heard
the black sounds flowing, slowly at first

—a battered goatskin, the string on a gourd . . .
then all we had to do (it seemed so easy)
was follow that music to its source.

SOURCE

Domes of clay burst in the clear depths
and trout hang in the upthrust of pure cold
in the pool where Arethusa rose for air
winding a Stygian rivulet through her head.

When Cicero was quæstor for Syracuse
he knew the tomb of Archimedes by
a circle enclosed inside a cylinder.
What was lost, then found, was lost again.

The port was whited marble, an island of ghosts.
I thought of the lupara bianca, the exact
diameter lodged in the sawn-off shaft
then the corpse vanishing in the white recoil.

The train wheels turned above the steel tangents.
The sea was mixing sand and sulphur and cement.
Tired, on either side of me: the emigrants
returning north again from their return.

lupara bianca: literally, 'white sawn-off shotgun' used to refer to
a mafia killing in which the victim disappears.

SIRENSONG

Why do you think he went on wandering
after the orchestrated pathos of his homecoming
—the hot bath, the clean sheets, the postal code?

It wasn't that he was bored by his wife;
more she by him and by those years of waiting
(for what?) with better prospects close at hand.

It wasn't as he pretended the desire
to travel to the edge of the known world
where he could found some godforsaken waste.

Lashed to the mast, did he think the wax
he'd also plugged his own ears with would work?
And that the siren's downcast eyes expressed

the fear she'd lost him not the lack of doubt
her voice would carry till it found him out?

SKIN DEEP

The headlamps of divers
cast a greasy cloud of light just under
the sea's dark skin. Before you can blink

the octopus has played a symphony
of russet stipples and black bands
across its back. It thinks in colour.

Beware and welcome have twenty inflections
like Delacroix saying Mon cher monsieur
—for tomorrow's lunch they'll all boil down

to an inky sauce, some Redon lithograph
of spiders dancing in the afterlife.

UROBOROS

I was partway outside a takeaway pizza napoletana
watching tv when the bone of an anchovy
stuck in my throat—a neat posthumous deterrent.
An eight-legged tag team tangled with the ropes
to the sound of squeezed ribs and pummelled rubber.
I switched to a thing on the mangrove swamps:
crabs eating muck, frogs eating crabs, snakes
eating frogs . . . so who eats the snakes? The snakes
eat themselves at the top of the food-chain
out of habit or boredom or sheer bravado.
It's a world of mud out there and you have to
like it to survive though even if you like it
no one's saying you survive for long.
What's that fish, the yokker fish or something,
that lurks and spits a crystal arc that knocks
the ants off overhanging blades of grass? There's no
safety in numbers, in looking insignificant or vile.
You can't say,—Don't mind me, I'm nothing special
and basically I taste of toenails. A taste for you
yoked to some gimmick for hunting you down
has been stalking through millennia intent
on the delicate dread of your last gasp.
It's a world of mud and guts out there. My advice
is don't be anything stupid like a shrimp
and evolve yourself a tooth- and claw-proof vest
and stay wedged deep in a burrow all your life,
if you call it a life, like the solitary mud lobster,
ugly as truth and glum as a lumpsucker
which seemingly without moving somehow keeps going
for it's a mystery how they get to mate.

FRANKENSTEIN'S PRE-NATAL
RECOLLECTIONS

The place of origin was emptiness
and fine metallic dust with lines
of bunsen burners burning nothing
or clearing their throats of filaments
and solder—blue-flecked black flames
sepulchral as cypresses. The air was utterly
exhaled, through-other like the name
we acquired, a cast-off from the doctor.
We thought we had been someone/something
else before, sought out like truffles
under lanterns and then swathed
in cellars; but that was before 'before'
and is a thought at best patched up.
Better to start with the gloomy angel
hunched over slide-rules and a rheostat
and those two galvanic shining spheres

fire linked—we felt fire stitch the air
and scatter filings in dark iron wings
and our heart leaped to the spark, one fell
precipitant connecting like Paganini
off on some solo. Our own right arm
which props our chin in this reflective mood
bears the pale papery stitched-up mark
of reaching through a glass door to escape
indoors, out of the agoraphobic garden
where rows of flowers array themselves
in threads not even Solomon . . .
but so unstriven-for we really wonder
what keeps them at it. For us each movement
is an impossible bridging of fault-lines,
each thought unprecedented as a tripod
which must learn to dance upon a tightrope.

STOOD UP

The clock turns bulbous, fisheyed, whiskery.
The longlegged clockhands take scissory strides
above you. Darts spring back from the jumbled dial,
pointedly snubbed, while you still wait

for a breathless explanation that would lift,
as a seal lifts a beachball, the dead weight
of your chin, of the hours, propped on your arm's
Dali stilt now that the clock has melted

in pools of spilt beer islanding the ashtray
and only the wind judders the swingdoors
or else some stranger. Half-stewed, old droopy-jaws

who winds the grizzled ends of his moustache
might well be you, but ten years on, still waiting
for love to walk in before closing time.

HE DRINKS PRECIOUS WINE WITH FLIES IN

Boorish flies equipped with dainty mouthparts,
dandruff scattered inside leather casks
that choose the crushed grape for your nemesis
as topsy-turvy moths are drawn to flame,

dome-headed midges, base-born atoms,
motes pissed as newts, seraphic soaks,
mites of the most prized vintages,
honey-bees in your pigskin hives,

wine-harvest ticks, you hurtle down the hatch
—your big eyes slipped the noose about your necks
but Bacchus carpentered your gallows;

with one more sip the rest of you sail down
to darkness . . . I drink you in a double-draught
of what you drank from first, then what you drowned in.

(after Francisco de Quevedo)

HOME THOUGHTS

The airmail from India, a weatherbeaten blue,
with wax marks from the candle you had used
to write by reached me. You write that reach
is what travellers there do rather than arrive
being more respectful to the gods of place.
For years your letters from around the world
have kept on reaching me wherever
I'm hunched beside an atlas and a lamp.
When you last saw me I was living in a room
across the road from but a floor below
the room we used to share ten years ago.
Only kindness stopped you saying
it took me quite some time to cross that road;
and looking from my window I expect to see
myself looking out to where in ten years time
I'll be looking back again to see . . . the last things
you mention are the Parsee towers of silence
where the dead are left for vultures to attend.
I warm to that. It sort of brings things home.

THE MASTER STROKE

for Xon de Ros

The hair stands on end and waits to be split
  by the heft of the little axeman.
The two halves peel the length of the hairshaft
to the applause of two ladies-in-waiting
whose calves are like four table legs.
The hair that's split is split again.
    That's not a hair the axeman says
it's a silk thread, a grass blade, the moth's antennae.

I dream at night beside the wedge-shaped tower,
  a glass axe buried in the earth.
Inside the column built inside the tower
they split a single atom into halves
then both halves have to spend their halflives
seeking the other half they'll never find.
    That's not an atom the axeman says
it's a misprint, a mutant, the mote in your eye.

suspicion

straight as a signpost
planted in space
the angel Uriel
kept watch on the heights

his four wings
of fiery quartz
made the glottal clack
of magpies or castanets

when asked which way
his arm replied
That spot to which I point
is paradise

and what if a devil
in passing had swivelled
his faithfulness
one eighty degrees

sleight of hand

just a sly shove
and the chipped angel
will plummet down
into the brambles

where I caught you
red-handed
with a bucketful
of blackberries

so that they fell
among your clothes
where there's time enough
for us to find them

hearing the bees tread
the sunflower's heart
their back legs
barrelled with gold

mortal remains

below the blue arrow
of the one way sign
above the harvest
of a street bin
the two tone
zinc
of a pigeon's wing
or Franciscan cassock
next to where a green
and ochre sticker depicting
a baffled rat declares
this street has been
deratted there's
a pale square
from which a funeral
poster has been torn
down leaving
only
a black border
with no lettering—
someone called something
Esposito
if I remember
right *was gathered up*
into the realm of angels

INHERITANCE

By prudence, integrity and diligence,
the Latin virtues, he had worked his way
from 'nothing' to those heights from which
it wouldn't take us long to fall. He left me
no blueprints and no climbing gear to haul
me back to solvency though I received
his christian name and surname
and dutifully plagiarized his signature
off the Isle of Man three-legged one-pound note.
Chief General Manager of Martins Bank:
his title had the decimal prestige
of a pentameter, of the rattle of beads
on an abacus, but was not hereditary.

I was however once invited to
the Liverpool Head Office, a temple
of trading ringed by gilded iron spikes
and the finial crochets of acanthus.
The manager led us down into the vault
where gold bars from Johannesburg were wheeled
about on trolleys; then up through a skylight
to the parapet above the dome. From there
the kingdoms of the city spread beneath us
rickety with fire escapes and aerials,
all blackened brick and base metals:
bombsites, dockyards, the Mersey's pimpled zinc.
Between us and nothing, the lowest of handrails.

The bank's emblem was a grasshopper
with backlegs triggered to unleash the bulk
of its blunt brow and plated thorax.
We had one as a gold paperweight poised
on a black plinth and another
squatting in the porch to prize off boots
with plaques of rust at its poll and wingcase.
Soon enough it would chirr in the crop of an eagle
when Barclays took over in a corporate merger.

Here there was a family history to be traced:
Martins had merged with the Bank of Liverpool
which years before in turn had joined
the firm of Arthur Heywood who had made
his pile from ships that plied the Gold
and Windward Coasts, Old Callabar, Benin . . .
a thousand leg-irons fixed to their quarterdecks,
those boats were christened with bright abstract names:
Integrity, Providence, Friendship, Liberty.

A SMALL FLAG

for Lucie Oldham

I'd barely finished painting and had meant to send
this mountain, less a mountain than a molehill
with a village at its foot and a village way up
but too faint to believe in, a hopeless idyll,

when news came of your death. The envelope
has stayed unstuck, unstamped, and void, and here,
now not one of your old addresses is any help
and no stamp on earth will see it past the border.

I thought of your arrival in Liverpool
in '68 when you entered the house as our new sister.
It was then I first heard of Dubček and Svoboda
and pinned a small enamel flag to my lapel.

You must have found our vicarious nationalism
quaint as a cloakroom, a far cry from Prague
and our lives by the oily river oddly tranquil
between the stolid hedge and the burgherly backwall.

Last time I saw you, in the restaurant,
you were thinner and paler, your eyes
unaltered and your voice a torrent
swerving between the disastrous and the humorous.

I still catch your accent, travelling backwards,
knocking the usual patterns of speech awry
to open meanings in the hearts of words,
ironic and mobile in their sleeves of air.

OXFORD POETS

Fleur Adcock
Kamau Brathwaite
Joseph Brodsky
Basil Bunting
Daniela Crăsnaru
W. H. Davies
Michael Donaghy
Keith Douglas
D. J. Enright
Roy Fisher
David Gascoyne
Ivor Gurney
David Harsent
Gwen Harwood
Anthony Hecht
Zbigniew Herbert
Thomas Kinsella
Brad Leithauser
Derek Mahon

Jamie McKendrick
Sean O'Brien
Peter Porter
Craig Raine
Henry Reed
Christopher Reid
Stephen Romer
Carole Satyamurti
Peter Scupham
Jo Shapcott
Penelope Shuttle
Anne Stevenson
George Szirtes
Grete Tartler
Edward Thomas
Charles Tomlinson
Chris Wallace-Crabbe
Hugo Williams